And Then He Kissed The Dog,
A Fine Break Up,
It Takes Two, One Is Not Enough

PAMELA SCHUYLER

ISBN 978-1-956010-22-0 (paperback)
ISBN 978-1-956010-23-7 (hardcover)
ISBN 978-1-956010-24-4 (digital)

Rushmore Press LLC
1 800 460 9188
www.rushmorepress.com

Printed in the United States of America

Cloudy With Blue Skies

I dedicate this book to all of us who need to understand the difference between reaction and response and to those who are capable of responding and forgiving.

CONTENTS

And Hollyhocks Bloom and Whither

INTRODUCTION

Breaking up and moving on.

The first thing you see is the mess and you actually think it looks good.

You see what has happened and you become overwhelmed.

Then you realize the relationship is over and this is real.

There is no way back.

As you stare into the mess that fills the space in your heart and mind you begin to understand that you have to let the relationship go.

It's like clearing out a house, overwhelming at first.

Then you remove one item at a time.

All of a sudden you have cleared out a drawer filled with memories, then a whole room.

Starting over again.

We wander through the journeys in our lives continuing to discover who we are slowly but surely.

We are works in progress, trying to understand our reactions and responses.

Trying to understand there are people who offer us inspirations and exasperations along the way.

We discover the most important relationship is with ourselves.

As we meet others on our journeys, with shorter and longer meets, some with joy, some with tears, our meetings help us grow into the people we are.

CHAPTER 1

INTROSPECTION

Many events were going on in my life during this new relationship; some things wrapped up the past and other events were part of my present life.

Events that were going on were dealing with my aging and dying mother's journey, moving from a memory-filled house to a new one, dealing with my aging and ailing dogs requiring continuous daily care and disturbed sleep nights, personal accidents and repairs from slipping on the ice, thousands of burning acres of forest near my new home where I needed to exit from the smoke-filled air to find my breath, continuing to teach yoga, my joy, and with smaller and larger events, including trying to find my someone. My life was more complex than I was aware of.

Through this, I tried to hang on to a close relationship with a new human being. I wanted and needed the simplicity of a new and exciting relationship with another.

But a new relationship is not simple because one is trying to work with another person who also has come from past experiences, and present challenges.

Many stress-filled issues needed resolution before I could thoroughly enjoy another.

The reality was I was asking a stranger for his support and in return, I was offering the stranger my support—a large responsibility for both of us. As older people come into a relationship, pasts that were built with others and incorporating the past experiences into a new relationship is nothing less than challenging that without commitment, it is impossible.

Taking on one's own responsibilities and incorporating another's life with one's own is a big job.

Is it possible to do? Yes, with openness, effort, compassion, and acceptance.

Sometimes, en route, we find another. Sometimes, it becomes a long-term partnership or a short-term adventure or learning experience.

Our life's journey continues with better understanding of who we are, our likes and dislikes, and what we can accept or not accept. With this understanding, two people join in partnership to learn from each other or part ways.

CHAPTER 2

DISCOVERING WHO WE ARE

Finding self.

In search of a relationship.

It takes one, then it takes two.

Then turbulence.

Relationships are tough.

Communication is necessary.

Sharing is integral

Respect is important.

Response and discussion is needed;

Reaction weakens communication.

If one doesn't talk about things that bother one, things cannot be fixed.

If one truly cares and is committed to another, there is sharing, there is discussion.

Explosions and storming off cause damage.

One person cannot see what is in another person's heart.

One person cannot see what is in another person's mind.

People have to work on imperfections in themselves and with their partners. This work becomes communication.

Commitment issues must be worked on with each other together, in person.

One must hear not just one's self but the other person; both individuals must listen with open heart and mind.

No judgment—just hear, listen, respond—don't react.

Men and women are different.

We all protect ourselves because of many years of independent living with self-protection from fear and from hurt.

Opening the door and letting someone in to expose who we really are requires trust.

Trust is being open.

Trust is being honest.

We must be bold and unafraid of discoveries about each other—good, bad, and neutral.

Getting hurt is no fun but is part of life.

Shutting down keeps love away making us less than we can be.

We do have different past experiences.

We do have baggage that has to be shared and accepted in order to love again.

We win by sharing, by being together, rather than being alone.

If one is a judge and a jury in a relationship, one doesn't want to solve problems.

If one wants to complain, one destroys.

When one assumes one understands without listening to the whole story, this person is just not interested in the truth.

Arrogance is when one thinks that only he or she has the right answers. These right answers have no room for discussion.

Expectations get us into trouble over time, yet expectations are inevitable the longer the relationship is.

CHAPTER 3

RELATIONSHIPS

I just cooked a squash from hell.
I never cooked a spaghetti squash before.
I baked it like other squash.
I put a fork in the skin to see if it was done.
The damn thing exploded in a big way—
Squash all over the kitchen, cabinets, floor,
oven interior, glass, me, orange, sticky string.
I never liked spaghetti squash before.
I don't think this event made me like it more.
The dogs didn't even assist in the cleanup.
They didn't look so good in orange and sticky.
I guess they don't like spaghetti squash either.
A mess.

CHAPTER 4

COMMUNICATIONS?

No response came immediately from my introspection.

I am hoping to find communication somewhere in this relationship.

Distant communication arrives, and I try to make sense of it in order to hold on to the relationship.

The response: "To rest is to rust. Rust is no movement and rain is not sitting still."

Hmm, I have to say rest is rejuvenation.

I think rest is not rust.

True, rain does not sit still, but rust is also movement—deterioration, breaking down.

An opera from two different worlds.

The disillusion? Destruction? Miscommunication happens with texting and emails and not being physically present to talk and observe each other's body language and tone.

My broken heart—not that two halves don't necessarily make a whole, though that has some truth in it too.

Is it foolish to try? My answer now is yes, it is foolish though not a waste of time for another learning experience.

CHAPTER 5

DESIRE TO UNDERSTAND
VERSUS UNDERSTANDING

There was a Christmas present with no Christmas—a gift that would allow two people to be together if they wanted to be together.

I returned the money to him for the gift he gave me. I liked the gift but did not want it to remind me of a broken relationship. He cashed the check, very practical on his part. His thoughtfulness was gone and kindness evaporated.

Holiday chaos happened.
Reasons why were never discussed.
Another brief interlude.
Another abrupt exit without explanation.

And I try to understand.
I have many guesses, many interpretations, but no explanation from this person.
I have always had a strong desire to understand.

My counterpart had a strong desire to be silent.

It is important for me to understand because I need closure. I laid all my cards out on the table and he kept his poker face.

Yes, living in the moment is important. Dealing with the moment comes from past experiences. Future responses and reactions are built on the present. Our memories do not fade and this moment comes from our histories and the future is created from the present.

I want to be part of the passage from past to present through the future with you.

My desire is to have our paths meet again one day over a glass of red wine with understanding and acceptance of what happened.

It seems I have always fought to be heard but the fight is wasted on someone who can't hear me.

Let it go.

When I look back, I felt my need to understand was ignored—I was not heard and my questions remained unanswered, which frustrated me, so my tolerance was pushed to the maximum, causing anger.

Upon further reflection, I really am not sure he was capable of exploring emotions and I did not understand this.

Can there be understanding, truth, and sharing when there is no resolution? No.

What made me so desirous of answers that I did not receive? It seems my needs were so strong I ignored the reality. Without answers from the other person, I continued to build on frustration which led to the explosion of anger. Let it go.

The problem was that the relationship was not all terrible. There were good things but unfortunately, over time, the good no longer outweighed the bad. The lack of communication was problematic for me. I tried to focus on those good things and I ignored my needs. This was not equitable.

I was trying to build on false hope thinking this person wanted to hear me and respond to me.

I think some of us do this because we believe that the truth within ourselves is so strong that it can be transmitted to others. This truth and caring have to live within each of us. When one tries to make someone hear what they choose not to hear, this causes the pain of futility. Let it go.

I thought I saw signs in the universe for the success of this relationship. We saw shooting stars, rainbows, full moon light, found objects on the beach in the shapes of hearts and fall colors. He said he saw the science of it all. I saw the romantic universe bringing us together. He did not. I tried to make him see me and our connection. He did not.

Now I understand. The universe shares with us the rainbows, full moonlight, the magic of stars in the sky, and the blooms in nature's garden. Even together, we are alone in this universe taking it all on.

Nature has given me a gift of smiles and a warm heart. We are alone, then sometimes together. The beauty of natural phenomena are the signs that connect me to the universe. These signs from nature are my reminders.

It doesn't have to be a sign that the universe wanted two beings to be together. It is just "what is."

Why did I feel I needed to work so hard? I believed in him.

I went downtown to pick up a gift I made for him.
The framed piece was chipped.
I waited for the repair.
I was hungry, so I ate at the diner next door.
My desire was to surprise him.
Boom, another land mine I did not see.
He walked out in anger and I did not understand.

CHAPTER 6

PHYSICAL HEALING

I got the MRI report. The doctor missed a fracture of the tibia which tore the meniscus. It took two months to get the MD to get me an MRI; this information was not seen in an X-ray.

I continued yoga and dog walking during this time with sharp burning pain in my leg. I was older. More time to heal—twelve weeks.

I can walk without support; just athletic tape. I still have swelling which comes and goes three years later. Yes, I can still ski with a brace, so I get support without doing more damage.

It seems like since my husband's death, I continue to lose my way.

I am so busy helping others I forget me. Sometimes, it seems easier that way. It really is not and my pain increases.

Definitely nice not holding up two people. It is less tiring.

I long for laughter and closeness. Perhaps, this makes me too eager to find someone.

I am working on selling the house my husband and I thought we would retire to. I need some space from memories.

I have difficulty accepting help from others because I have always been independent.

Perhaps I am concerned if I accept help, it won't be there when I need it again.

Is it a lack of trust? Yes.

Here I am, continuing to find my way.

CHAPTER 7

COMPANIONSHIP

Mom looks good at 101. She is slower though and not as sharp; I caught her drifting briefly into history. She is letting go of material things.

He showed up on my text again.
How are you?
How is your knee?

Here I go again, being drawn into my feelings for him. My vulnerability makes me weaken because I remember the good stuff and I miss his companionship.

I hope someone will listen to me, hear me, and understand me, not try to fix me. The blues come in and go out.

I responded; I just saw a movie worth seeing. You know when we talked yesterday, you made me cry when you told me about the beautiful trip you took with your ex-wife.

I was so looking forward to traveling with my husband after he retired and I waited . . . Now, I have to travel by myself.

I do miss companionship; I do miss your companionship. You are fortunate to have those memories.

I think that by way of your talking, you like taking care of someone. I like taking care of someone too and being taken care of. Can we take care of each other?

The answer was we can take care of each other but only for a short time within this relationship.

I continue; it is so difficult to trust someone after so many years of distancing, but I would like to try.

I hope you can open your heart again and enjoy each other's company for a longer time rather than a shorter time.

I know it is easier for you to talk about your family rather than yourself.

I guess I wanted to talk about you with you so I could enjoy your voice, discovering who you are. But I know this upsets you and you shut down.

The key is working with each other in a relationship so it becomes you and me, so it becomes we. A general someone is a thought, imaginary, and not in the present.

CHAPTER 8

COMMUNICATION

He texts, hi, my mom passed away at 99+, she threw in the towel; rapid decline within weeks.

He sent me her obituary, birthdate, schooling, description of her as a wife, homemaker, grandmother, her profession, liked social events, her being an avid reader, traveler, and who she was survived by—family—children, grandchildren, great-grandchildren, etc.

Interestingly, I attended church services the night of her departure. As the scriptures were read, I asked the minister to bless your mom when you hadn't yet told me of her passing. I asked for your mom's healing so she could pass in peace.

Interesting our lives' connections on different levels.

With health for all on many levels.

With healing on many levels.

With love and compassion on many levels.

Peace.

If you need to say something out loud, I am here.

I changed the subject to move us back to the conversation.

Next, I begin to talk about my mending leg. I took a four-mile hike with the boys (my dogs) yesterday. Definitely improving and up to four miles on the stationary bike.

My physical therapist offered some good stretching exercises.

He texts, it sounded like a good session.

He tells me his mouth is recovering. He is on the last of his antibiotics today.

He will cleanse his body with wine . . . alcohol, good antiseptic, tastes good too.

We are a pair.

I like the anesthesia idea. I can use it for physical therapy, ha, ha, cheers.

Do stay hydrated 1:2 or three glasses of water to a glass of wine.

Just made meatballs and spaghetti.

Ciao.

Guess which anesthesia I chose? Italian (smile).

He commented:

But . . . you doze off after anesthesia.

And I am and I have.

He comments good night. Sweet dreams.

My response:

Zzzzzzzzz

Happy trails.

The next morning, I need answers . . .

Howdy.

Three questions:

1. What specifically makes you unavailable?
2. What are you specifically looking for in a relationship other than wanting someone active and healthy?
3. What are serious turnoffs in a relationship?

He responds:

3. One who is interested in talking about ex-spouses.
2. Intelligent, sexy.
1. Being turned off.

He added:

4. Why is it difficult for couples to share the cost of "stuff?"

I respond to his answers:

4. It shouldn't be difficult to share the cost. In fact, it is nice. Special event treats are the exceptions.
3. Why is it a turnoff to discuss ex-spouses when one wants to avoid mistakes in a new relationship—when I want to avoid a landmine?

He goes back to question 3 sharing a discussion about a date he had which he felt included inappropriate ex-mate discussion. On this occasion, he went on and said, I sat and listened to "how great shape her, dead husband was in." He said he should have just gotten up and left.

I am glad you did not leave.

Compassion is kindness.

Being rude seems to be an everyday occurrence. Some people are mostly selfish and only think of themselves.

Listening to someone may even include pleasant discoveries.

I do enjoy texting with you but prefer in-person dialogue.

Are you sure it wasn't three balls instead of three strikes referring again to his exit?

It is funny how someone who wants to live in the present, enjoys good dialogue, is intelligent, compassionate, and sexy doesn't understand why people need to learn from the past so they can move on.

I think you miss opportunities to enjoy someone's company and presence in the moment.

He says he does not know what to say; we already discussed this issue. *Unfortunately, I did and he did not participate fully.*

I respond, no worries, it was in my heart and mind, got it out, feel better.

But with an unanswered question at this moment, my feelings are stuffed in the back of my heart and mind, causing a buildup of unheard expressed feelings.

You just happen to make my heart beat fast and I just want more.

Too many Hallmarks in the past, says he.

Yet he won't admit he cries at Hallmark movies and always buys Hallmark cards.

Sadly, every time he gives me a Hallmark card with loving thoughts, he runs away.

At least you made me realize I still enjoy being close to someone.

There are so many different types of relationships: relationships with one's self—mentally, physically, and spiritually; relationships with friends, family, lovers, spouses, siblings, acquaintances, the universe, and God.

In this day and age, relationships online with texts and emails make contact vaguer.

But here we are trying to be part of something. We want to sustain ourselves with human contact.

Texting is a conversation one letter at a time and an exercise in patience. It can be communication, confusion, or miscommunication. However, this can become more and more challenging in times of isolation. Computer communication doesn't allow us full communication with someone. It is partial and can create confusion and misunderstanding. In pandemic times, how do we cope alone?

In Buddhist thought, relationships with others both long-term and short-term are passing.

Our chief relationship?

It is with ourselves as part of the universe.

CHAPTER 9

MOM

Visiting my mother, I sent him a text after we stopped seeing each other.

Getting old without independence is awful.

Please make sure this doesn't happen to either of us.

My mother can't see her food.

She eats with her fingers.

She can't hear well and yet, I still love her.

He reminds me that she still recognizes me!

True. She cannot see me even when I am nose to nose. In a way, I guess that is a plus because she can't see me enough to criticize my hair or what I am wearing!

She can't really hear either; I have to speak loudly which I do not like doing.

She laughs when I say "fuck it!" In the older days, she couldn't even say the word.

Did your mom know who you were until the end?

He said yes, his mom was coherent until the end, but her body imploded the last few months. Yes, she was coherent but had substantially lost hearing, mostly blind, and had serious arm tremors.

Both moms seemed to approach old age and death in a similar fashion.

My mom still has her appetite—she just ate three pieces of salmon on a bagel with red pepper, two black olives, potato salad, and coleslaw! She fingered it with gusto! She said the food at independent assisted living is disappointing.

I am not sure whether that is true. She does like to complain.

His text support continues, how are you holding up?
When are you heading to NYC?

I will be leaving Monday afternoon for New York City. I am very stressed out, lots of drama, but I am holding up.

My continued saga—

The guest room at mom's complex is not great.

I just spoke with the antique dealer who sold her household items. Today, he is pleasant enough. I hope he offers her a check; he has been procrastinating for two years.

Mom wants to see an itemization of her things; I doubt that will happen.

I do hope she gets something. It is better than nothing. I hope I can make something happen.

It could be a serious stalemate. Mom has no idea what a mess she left in her home and what they had to clean out in order to find what was sellable.

He agreed it would be a shame if she can't get some money.
Again, he asks how I am.

My response was, how am I? Om. (A meditation sound trying to maintain my calm.)

He says oh my god.

I tell him he is blessed to have siblings to have shared his mom's endgame with.

Again, he comments somewhat, sometimes. Be strong.

You stay strong too. Whew, sometimes, one just needs a hug. I have done hospice work, but . . . tonight, I feel so alone, sad, maybe even fearful, which I know is useless. Fear only stops things.
I know this will pass.
Do appreciate your response.

He sends me a hug.
And wishes me sweet dreams.

I will try.
Gotta find a Hallmark Movie Channel.
Great, fake TV in this room.
I hope the bed is real.
This room is bad.

He comments, that sucks but I hope the price is right.

Mom is paying for this visit.
Great, no blankets.
I am going down to the front desk.
Jeez, no trash can either.
No dishes in the kitchen.
No phone.
I am going to find the front desk now.

He replies, perhaps a motel room would be better.

Great, I am lost in the maze of hallways.

I am in luck, I just met a woman with a search and rescue dog (grin). They helped me find the front desk. She agreed the hallway layout is confusing.

I will crash here tonight.

I have been up since 3 a.m.

He said, you sound tired.

I am.

I am sending you sweet dreams when I get back to the room.

I just finished off the champagne I shared with mom.

Going for the Zzzzzz's.

Nite.

He pulled a muscle in the back of his leg yesterday; he is icing it now.

Hope you got a good night's sleep, he texted.

Going to do a short hike this a.m. Hope not one-legged!

I think sometimes, heat works better if the injury is not inflamed to get the circulation going.

He agreed he likes heat too and says he will apply heat after his breakfast.

I opened the window last night. There was no heat in the room either. When I woke up, I was very cold.

I was sound asleep and security walked in to see if I needed anything.

Great privacy!

I think I will check out a motel around here before I run out of toilet paper!

An almost ha, ha.

Walk into a place like this and you give up the right to die.

My new profession is a stand-up comic.

His comment: snow in the forecast.
Enjoy your day.

I respond, she is clicking the heels of her ruby slippers that get me home; there is no place like home.

He texts, skiing starts this weekend near where you live.
He thought it was the first ski weekend. The mountain had an opening party downtown.

I am keeping the refrigerator door open to keep warm!
Is old age contagious?
Send another hug. Urgent!
Aaaaargh!

He: Hug going your way.
Had a nice hike today with my friend.

I see burgers in your future!

He: My friends are taking off to Hawaii.
No burgers tonight.
Pizza!
Hang in there, missy.
He asks, did you get a motel room? Or did you decide to rough it?

I have been running around for mom like crazy.
I am camping out again.

He tells me to enjoy. Can you lock the door?

I respond, no worries, I left most of my stuff in the locked car rental.
Security and maintenance have full access.
How's the leg?

He says his leg is good.

The heat, cold, and hike seemed to help.

He then asked how my hand appointment went. *(In the middle of all of this, I am recovering from a dog bite).*

The doctor thinks the dog bite triggered arthritis. I don't buy it.

Personally, I think it's still a local infection that is stuck. From my Eastern medical training, this rings true and as it turned out, my hand was healed after one year.

Animal control still has not responded, still has no report, I don't get it.

He suggests, why don't you call and speak to the mayor!

Why should I do that? I reply.

Animal control works for her.

Me: Can you believe it? The mayor herself actually picked up the phone and said to call the city manager's office.

Thank you for the advice.

I am going back to see mom before I get fired!

Take care.

I am moving to a hotel.

He comments, that's a good idea!

Just spoke with rug guy who will come by after Thanksgiving to evaluate my rugs.

I know you have been curious about their value.

Police gave me directions and a phone number for animal control.

I left a message and shortly thereafter, received the report. *(My small dog and I were attacked by a big dog who jumped out of a parked car while I was walking them downtown; very scary.)*

Finally, success.

He said, happy you finally received the report from animal control.

It turns out dinner is not pizza, but it is Italian, using the microwave cooker. It makes perfect pasta.

And a glass of red.

Our texts are flying back and forth—a challenge to keep up with so many thoughts.

I just got two warm chocolate chip cookies at the front desk and a tall milk—a sedative offering from the hotel management, which was greatly appreciated.

Your ravioli looks interesting. Sounds good with red.

Tonight, I am a needy human who needs yet another hug.

Delicious cookies with walnuts too.

He sends several xoxo's to me!

Whew, I needed that.

Wow, ravioli looks fabulous out of the package.

Restaurant style.

How's the wine?

He tells me the wine is good and continues, 30% off if you buy six bottles at the market.

I texted I saw *Wonder Woman* on the plane, I liked it.

Cookies and milk are dinner for me at the hotel. No dinner service here.

He replies, I liked *Wonder Woman* too.

Just saw *Loving Vincent*, another really good movie.

The morning arrived; I comment, lazy morning for me.

He replies, you are in a very stressful situation; lazy is good. And makes time for you. Hope your day goes well.

Thanks, I said. It was another tough day.

Mom was crying about her endgame.

She signed the POLST (physician orders for life sustaining treatment). This was a big step for her because I do not think she ever thought she would die.

She wanted me to take over her finances.

This independent, stubborn woman is seeing her endgame.

She said I may never see her alive for the next trip.

Not like her . . .

I paid her current bills.

She is letting go.

I had her in my arms like a baby as she cried.

Oh, dear sir.

What you went through when your mom moved on.

I am so happy you had siblings and son support. You are blessed. This is a rough trip.

I am going to bed. It is in the 20s tonight.

(Most of my family is gone, ahh, getting older. I certainly appreciated communicating with him.)

He saw the opera. He said there were not enough performances.

He then said my ski mountain had enough snow for opening day skiing, with no green trails open.

I am getting knee braces to support the injured knee when I get home. The braces are well designed. I will be ready to ski with stability and confidence in both knee joints.

Tomorrow, he texts, perhaps a hike and then . . .

Taos and Santa Fe skiing are a few weeks off.

I found a crumb cake at the supermarket.
I use to eat crumb cake as a kid; comfort food tonight.
Help!
I need to step back from the crumb cake!
The crumb cake is so good.
And the ballet, how was it?

He describes the ballet as an interesting behind-the-scenes flick.
He said, OMG you really made a dent in the cake.

I reply, the ballet sounds good.
Okay, I am closing the cake lid—stepping back, walking away.
I am so full.
But it got me out of the blues.
Probably won't eat until dinner tomorrow.
Burp!
Think I ate for three.
Oh well.

Oh, The Crumb Cake!

What did you have for dinner? He asked.

I had some hand-sliced smoked salmon, olives, and said in a whisper, a humongous piece of crumb cake.
By the way, sweets are not my usual. I am a salt person.
And you, what did you have for dinner? I asked.

He had a salad with chicken and beer.

Well done, sir.
My next question, what will you wear on the mountain? Ha, ha.

Not sure, need to get stuff out of the storage chest.
Will pick boots and skis up at the tune-up store tomorrow.

The chitchat kept my mind off my mother's chaos and my loneliness.

He is going to spend Christmas week in New Jersey with his brother- and sister-in-law.

Very nice, I say.

He said his brother wanted him to come on Thanksgiving, but it was too close to get reservations.

I ask him to enjoy his visit.

He thanks me and says he also plans to visit NYC.

I say, great, and will you also visit with your cousin you like?

He said he will if he is available.
Again, he asks, when I am heading to NYC.

I am leaving mom's place tomorrow afternoon.

He responds, enjoy yourself.

I respond, thank you, and continue . . .

I know this is above and beyond the call of duty, but I really could use someone to speak with. Do you have a moment now?

I appreciate this.

I am back at the hotel.

I got rid of a lot of Mom's things today so Mom's aides won't fall over her piles of stuff she has purchased from television shows.

Mom did a lot of yelling and crying.

This is really, really difficult.

I am exhausted. I still have to do bank chores for her in the morning.

The antique dealer bailed.

Mystifying. Not sure what to do about that.

I hope the ballet was splendiferous.

Thanks again for listening.

(I got pretty beaten up with mom. She lived another two years. It took two more years after that to straighten out her affairs. As a dutiful daughter, I did just that. Her financials were resolved including resolution with the antique dealer while she was still alive.)

He answers, the ballet was great.

Does the antique guy owe her money?

Yes, he cleared out mom's house; he probably owes a substantial amount of money. She was waiting for almost two years. He promises, then bails with health excuses for him or someone else.

I spoke with mom's lawyer yesterday.

I haven't spoken to her lawyer since he bailed.

Let's chat tomorrow.

(I didn't catch the pattern for quite some time. Never now, always later. It felt as if I was always being put off. This made me feel I was unimportant in his life.)

He suggests, call your mom's lawyer. Have him send a letter demanding payment by a certain date. If he doesn't pay, take him to court.

I just left mom's lawyer the message.
Thanks.

A possibility, he says, the statute of limitations may apply.

Lord and Taylor's Christmas Window Display

CHAPTER 10

HOLIDAY!

Jersey girl in New York City!

Any reprieve for an ex-Jersey girl who gained wisdom? I asked him, missing his company.

Carnegie Deli is closed, what is the world coming to?

He joins in the talk; that is a shame Carnegie Deli is closed. Let's chat tomorrow a.m.

(I should have realized he was just trying to be nice, but no longer wanted to be with me. I pushed because I needed him and wanted him to need me. I was my worst enemy because I couldn't accept "what is.")

I am feeling the effects of my glass of wine from my restaurant dinner.

I am taking a cab back to the hotel.

He greets me the next day with good morning *(This day is a lazy day for him.)*.

I comment, you? Lazy?

He continues, he is conserving energy for Thanksgiving and Christmas.

Tomorrow, he goes to the gym and completes a five-mile hike. He says he is keeping in shape for NYC; lots of walking to be done in the city.

Yup, I agree and with all of the eye candy, it is easy to walk and walk.

I forgot it is so much earlier where you are.

That is true, he says.

I went to an old haunt, a west village restaurant I haven't been to for thirty years.

It hasn't changed. The same owners. Good ratings. Tonight, manicotti and a good red. Salut!

He says it looks like a beautiful evening. Yum *(I took him there the following year)*. He says turkey for me tonight.

He tells me he picked up his skis and boots and plans on going on a hike.

The NYC Dinner

Bergdorf Goodman's Christmas Window Display

I just bought the poodles new wool sweaters.

The cashmere ones were too pricey.

I continue, it is dark here.

I took the bus today; traffic was crazy because of the Thanksgiving Day parade tomorrow. Many streets are blocked off.

I am leaving early tomorrow before the parade begins.

Mom is enjoying my NYC stories.

Since she can't see me anyway, I have no guilt about not being with her. She can crank up the sound on her cellphone and hear me!

He says his skis are tuned and married to his boots.

Congrats, health and joy.

I can see you getting picked up on the slopes, I mean by a gorgeous lady, not the ski patrol!

For me, Zabar's bounty and reward, just love that New York Deli!

Rye bread is still warm.

Next up, gallery visit.

Then Bergdorf Goodman's Christmas windows. They are weird and extraordinary!

There was a great Judith Dench movie at the Paris Cinema.

Oh, the rye bread from Zabar's, she is swooning.

He comments oh, how the mighty have fallen!

I haven't fallen, just different priorities! (smile)

Oh, The Rye Bread!

Bergdorf Goodman's Christmas Window Display

Lord and Taylor's department store windows haven't lost their Christmas window magic either.

More chitchat.

Another comment from this woman's perspective.

A trophy human is someone that can walk shoulder to shoulder, hand-in-hand with beauty inside and out, in the morning and in the evening and at night, really enjoying supporting a man she is with and having him support her via emotions, joy, and physical closeness. Now, that's a trophy.

He doesn't respond to my thoughts but replies that he is looking forward to seeing the displays when he goes at Christmas for his family visit *(I would have liked to have been with him.).*

Me: The wool sweaters are gorgeous and handknitted too!

The poodles have arrived stylin' New York City boys!

I enjoyed the texts so much I asked again if there was any chance to get back together again. I truly missed him.

(Even when we stopped seeing each other, we continued texting. I needed someone and he responded. I was needy, sigh. I took the crumbs. I needed more but accepted crumbs.)

So, multiple choice answers to my question, can we get back together again?

a. No way.

b. Maybe.

c. Absofuckinlutely.

Since you like 4 questions and answers, I add—

d. When hell freezes over.

(He did not respond and I thought we were having so much fun chatting.)

I even love the traffic in NYC, I must be turning into a tourist!

It has been a long time since I was here, maybe 10–15 years.
Heading to Fifth Avenue.

The relationship with him seemed to be a distraction from myself, not an acknowledgment of myself or an acceptance of all my needs.

He sends good wishes.
Enjoy the day.
He is off to the talk show. *(More frustration for me because I wanted to hear he wanted to be with me; I couldn't accept "what is.")*

I hope you have good questions to answer on the radio show.

He commands, put your phone away; enjoy NYC!

I say it's better when you share.

His next comment, Charlie Rose got fired!

You just told me not to look at my phone.
What happened?
I forgot that NYC fabulous energy!

Rose sexually harassed women; at least eight women have come forward. He apologized.
He then called me, your mailbox is full. I could not leave a message.

Ok, I cleared voicemail.
How was the talk show?
I am looking forward to your call.
I went to a great Greek restaurant 1/2 block from the hotel. Delicious.

Saks Fifth Avenue Light Show

Saks Fifth Avenue had an amazing light show and fireworks!
Ahh, the wine.

Good night.

He sends me a good night.
The radio show went well.

I made it out of the NYC parade maze.
My flight is in two hours.
Enjoy Thanksgiving.

He asks, did you take off yet?

Not yet, I reply.
Plane snooze for me.
I left NYC at 5 a.m.
Arrived home 5:02 p.m.
I can't get to sleep.
I keep checking the clock.
When is your turkey dinner?

CHAPTER 11

THANKSGIVING

I am finally in the same time zone as you are.
Home sweet home, yeah.

He boasts of his multiple Thanksgiving invites—two dinners today, one last night.
Belt loosening coming up.
Last Thanksgiving, he said he was with his family.

I comment it is amazing that single men are so popular for invites.

He continues, that he is on his way for a five-mile hike.

I am picking up the poodles tomorrow.
Looking forward to seeing them.
I hope their new sweaters keep them warm this winter.
I am opening a bottle of wine, an excellent vintage from California—we did enjoy it. Do you remember?

He says yes he does.

I went to a friend's house for Thanksgiving. My responsibilities were cranberry sauce and pies.

Yikes, I burnt the cranberry sauce so I added bourbon. No one knew. Heh, heh.

What were you thinking about when you were cooking the sauce?

I was opening the sliding glass door to let some air in and the door jammed so I called the repair person and was put on hold. I had to go to another room for better reception and forgot the sauce. The stove was a mess.
The result, bourbon cranberry sauce. My new invention! I am driving carefully.

He said he never tried that.

I ask how were the turkey dinners?

He texts turkey good.
Company better.
On my way home now.

Glad you had great Thanksgiving dinners.
Thanks for the tire chain information.
Night.

He wishes me a good night.

I am walking the poodles.
I have a 7 a.m. yoga class to teach.

Enjoy, he replies.
Off to the gym shortly.
How was your yoga class?
He had a good workout.
He just finished with the talk show. The show was excellent.

He continues, thinking about buffalo sliders for dinner and a beer!

Wish I could join you for a beer—cheers.
(Always wished he would invite me to be with him regularly to share a good meal with him. I so enjoyed the closeness.)
Spent all day going nowhere on the internet.
Apparently, it is my new cellphone's improved service (sarcasm).
The next time you email or call will be the test.
What were the radio show topics you discussed?

He lists the topics.

Right up your alley. I would like to hear this one.

He said he would send me the link.

I made turkey the day after Thanksgiving so the dogs and I could enjoy leftovers.
We overate the turkey.
I am putting the rest in the freezer.

He sent me a photo of the desert he ate.

A good-looking cake.
I said it was perfect for sharing.

He commented, all gone.
You need to work some of that turkey off.
Walk the dogs.
Sweet dreams.

I offer good wishes of good sleep to him as well.

The next day, he wishes me a good morning. He is on his way to yoga.

I say, enjoy.

His next mission—the dentist.

Anesthesia for you.
My response to a question he asked:
Viny yoga from Sanskrit, vinyasa yoga which is a continuous flow exercise.
I found a good nurse practitioner here for an annual physical.
One of my clients recommended a great arboretum in Dallas, Texas. Sounds like a good place to explore when NYC weather is nasty.
I mention, don't forget to fill out the POLST documents, keep one in the medicine cabinet, one in the vehicle, and one in the travel suitcase.
Is your temporary crown done yet?

He talks about vitamins. He takes D3 and K2.
His vitamin D count increased after regularly taking 5,000 units of D.

My radiant heat boiler is being installed now, finally.

He greets me good morning, just finished breakfast.
Had world-class grits and eggs.
Enjoying coffee.

Sounds good. I am fasting for blood work.

So, the dialogue continued for several years. It was joyous chatter about small things with humor, politics, sadness, confusion, and frustration. I was trying so hard for the closeness to work at a distance. There were interludes of being in the same city. We tried and we did not try—another variation of a relationship.

I was ready to give it my all but he locked his feelings away and never allowed me to stay close for any length of time. He was able to compartmentalize all of his relationships in his mind. He would give me no clue as to how we could maintain a good relationship.

The buildup of confusion with his lack of explanation created frustration to distancing. The focus of closeness turned into distancing and moving on.

CHAPTER 12

CUTE

The dogs were lazy this morning, I had to wake them up for a walk. Would you like a couple of lazy poodles as guide dogs for your hike?

Of course, he said, yes.

The boys will meet you on your five-mile creek trail hike.
You will recognize them with their red wine emergency kegs at their necks.
I thought I gained weight with all that Thanksgiving crumb cake. Turns out I lost 7 pounds. I think I discovered the best diet ever!
The poodles are still searching for you. You returned without the poodles!

He enjoyed the hike and my humor—cute.

Here is my brace for skiing. I sent a photo.

He says nice leg; brace too.
Ski mountain is opening on the ninth.

My information—minimal snow here at home.
Mountain bike/ski combo up the mountain.

Off for a walk.

I will have to check out your mountain one of these days.

I noticed he is quiet today. How is your new phone?

He says his phone is good.

He just got home.

Good night. Sweet dreams. Sleep well.

You too.

I just think we need to say good night to each other and not eat too much, too late.

When do the town Christmas lights go up? I heard they are lovely.

He says he had a nice hike, then went out to dinner with the gang.

Christmas decorations are up around town now.

I reply, there is a full moon soon. The dogs and I are perfecting our howling techniques.

I went to the local craft show.

Enjoy.

Sleep tight and don't let the bed . . . bite.

And to you, sweet dreams.

Good morning.

Hope you slept well.

He said, so-so.

He feels good.

He wishes me a glorious day.

He is working out at the gym. He mentions he will call back around 10.

My gang took me to a glass blowing event and craft fair. I will talk to you later when I get home.

My phone failed after the phone company changed passwords. Good night.

Good night, missy.

Tomorrow, I have a court appointment for the dog attack case after yoga.

He tells me nothing to fear except fear itself.

I took a nap and had a bad dream.

He asks, what is bad?

My dream was of a death mask of mom.

He responded—ugh!

I agree, truly, ugh!

He says a hug is coming my way.
He says he was restless too.
Full moon coming tonight.
He is about to take a nap himself.

I hope he has a better dream!

Later that evening, I text I am going to have to pause the Hallmark station. I am running out of tissues.

Hey you, I am concerned about you taking western medicine sleeping aids for sleep. After he mentioned he had trouble sleeping, I suggested using turmeric and milk and doing breathing exercises, inhale full breath from belly to upper chest, exhale breath to belly gently pressing belly toward spine five rounds or so. This keeps the mind strong and will relax you much better than a sleep aid.

Thinking about you, xoxo.

Nite, nite. Peaceful sleep.

He replies, nite, nite with many sweet dreams.

The next morning, I wished him a good morning and said I was getting ready for yoga. I asked him how he slept.

He said it was windy here this morning.

Not from the breathing exercises!

He said he would call later in the a.m.

Just thinking that I should have invited you up for the court hearing. I would have liked your observations.

He assures me that everything will be fine.

Here I go, off to court. The dog owner did not show. The judge will have to re-schedule.

If he doesn't show next time, the dog's owner will receive a bench warrant.

This court stuff is wasting my time.

Poodles are sound asleep.

He asks later in the evening if I will be skiing the next day.

My response was no because my skis were not tuned yet and I have to teach yoga.

Before bed, he wishes me a good night with sweet dreams of sugar plums and healed knees xoxo.

Chamber meeting today, then yoga.

He responds, enjoy your day.

I reply, you too.
Yoga was good. My body felt rusty today.

He: Use some oil.

A quote from our teacher, Dr. Vasant Lad:

"*In reality, our daily life is full, complete, total, and abundant. It is really a gift. We should express gratitude to the life-giver who gives us life.*

If we look around, people are not really happy; they are always thinking in terms of should be, could be, and would be. They cannot face what is.

'What is' is what you are: fear, anger, love, compassion.

'What is' is not permanent. It is just for the time being.

'What is' is here to guide us. The moment 'what is' comes to the surface, we have a name for it.

By naming what is makes it distorted.

Look at 'what is' with great awareness and give complete freedom to it. Just let it flower.

When 'what is' resolves into abundance, you will appreciate and express gratitude toward anger, sorrow, and grief. No one else can transform you; only 'what is' can do this.

The real guru is 'what is.' Your guru is within you. This is the innermost journey of 'what is.'

What should be, what could be, what would be is an idea, an illusion, and we always pursue this illusion.

The real gratitude, the real fulfillment, the real abundance is within the heart of 'what is.'"

Hot Air Balloons Floating By

The elk were everywhere the night before and he asks in the morning if there were any more elk around.

It's too dark to see.
The ducks are quacking up a storm.
All is quiet. Everyone is at church.
Hot air balloons are floating over my house.
Last year, I would have been skiing. This year, I don't even need a jacket to walk the dogs.

Got it.
How is the move down the mountain progressing?

Most stuff in the house can now be donated or thrown out. Need a truck to get one large piece down.
I can let go of most clothes. Need someone to say just let it go.
One of the dogs ran off. I found him hanging out at his buddy's house.
Currently, he is under house arrest.
How is your day going?

He replies ok, full moon last night, very restless.
Had a nap.
Watching skiing on TV. It is overcast now, it feels like rain. I am going to a lecture on human rights . . .
The lecture was not very good. Too lopsided.
How was your day?
Looking forward to hearing about your day.

It was a good chamber meeting, I said. I packed more stuff.
Walking the poodles. Then sweet dreams.
Hope you are tucked in safe and sound.

He says he will be.

Just chilling out. Enjoy your walk. Night missy.

The next day, he wishes me a good morning.

It is a beautiful day.

Snow is in the forecast here.

(I had so many things going on and I was so unsettled. He comforted me.)

Good morning, dear sir.

It is fresh and crisp here. A glaze of ice on the pond.

I have fifteen minutes to talk before I take off for class if you want to talk.

He mentions he just finished his work out and asks me to call him when I am finished teaching.

He then asks if I am free?

I will call after class.

I am so excited. I found a coffee shop that sells the NY times on Sunday. I will get there at 7 a.m. to pick up a paper and see the ad for my new book. Feels like a wonderful celebration.

(I would have enjoyed sharing this with him in person; he never even commented on my enthusiasm.)

Finally, he finds a homeopathic natural sleep aid his doctor says is effective rather than the western medicine sleep aids.

He is going to check it out at a local health food store.

(In my thoughts, I was always hoping we can do these things together one day—would-have, could-have, should-have thoughts—not accepting "what is" and this is the root of my sadness.)

The next day, I wish him a good morning.

File cabinets came today.

Ready to fill them.

He responded that he was restless last night because he got to bed too late.

———— ∾ ————

CHAPTER 13

HOUSE CLEAR OUT

It is cold here. The dogs and I had a short walk. Light snow as well.

Yoga was good.

I am heading to breakfast.

Going through stuff in the garage—why am I keeping this stuff here? What do I have to shred?

He returned my phone call but the mailbox was full and he could not leave a message.

What a waste of time. I have been on the phone with the phone company for three hours; nothing works.

He says he is shopping and will call me when he gets home.

He tells me to delete some of my voicemail.

I let him know I am eating out tonight.

He sends hugs!

Call when you get home.

Are you home yet?

I am heading down the mountain now.

He comments he misses radiant heat at his house and his feet feel cool. He is heading to bed to warm up.

You are so cute. Hugs.

Have sweet dreams.

Me: Poor kid, foot rub?

Shredding records.

He: Have fun.

Off to the gym.

Once again, I am off to walk the mighty poodles, then back to the garage to continue packing for my move down the mountain.

Countdown to Sunday New York Times ad.

Congratulations sir, you made it to the mountain first. Use that core. Warm hugs all the way down the mountain.

For me, progress in the garage, signs of the floor.

Too much lifting, lower back sore.

A cold compress will do the trick.

Escaped to a chamber meeting.

He continues the chat and says he is dining with his ski gang. A dozen folks showed up. It was a nice evening.

I look forward to hearing about skiing, trees, and bumps; enjoy my dear.

A shooting star—I thought it was another sign for us.

Good luck with your boots. Night. Sweet dreams.

He says his boots are a work in progress.

He will be at his house in ten minutes and will talk to me soon.

Having turmeric tea tonight. Letting it brew for fifteen minutes.

Excellent. I will have some too.

I am writing a few Christmas cards.

Are you lighting candles?

Yes.
He is saying the prayer.

This warms my heart.
Good night.

And sweet dreams to you too.
Happy Hanukah.

Me: Thank you.
The next day I asked if he called.

He: Pocket call. Getting boots fixed. Success.
Boots tweaked.
The salesman still wants me to be in a smaller boot.
Nothing worse than sloppy boots on blacks.

Me: In the old days when I was skiing blacks, my boot buckles
popped open—yard sale. Need loose toes and tight heels.

Christmas Lights

CHAPTER 14

CHRISTMAS AROUND THE CORNER

He texts me he is reading.

He is having a beer with spinach soufflé for dinner.

He talks about his New Jersey departure and his flight schedule.

(With all his support with my mom, he accepted my offer of thanks by letting me drive him to the airport to visit his family. We will get to see each other again.)

He tells me about the Christmas lights in town, his plans for skiing, then he continues that he is heading home for a cleanup.

Drive safe.

Night missy.

I mention one of my friends who works up the mountain said to stay away because of so little snow. People are getting shoved into the dirt while skiing.

Sounds like accidents waiting to happen.

Instead, yoga today.

Making spare ribs and mashed potatoes today.

He says, sounds good.

Train Ride

He is going to be at the gym and describes his breakfast and of course, coffee.

Then, he wishes me a good morning.

He texts that he will call me back in ten minutes.

I mention to him that I have a house guest and as my role as a tour guide, we are off for a train ride.

His response is that he is still waiting for the roofer, then the ski hill.

I will be at a downtown restaurant this evening. My guest and I gabbed until late. Next, we are going up the mountain—dog sledding.

I ask him if he is happy with how the roofer handled the job.

My guest's departure is tomorrow.

Mom is calling in a panic. One of her aides went to visit her daughter out of town for three weeks and mom is freaking out with the substitutes. She has been calling and calling since 7:10 a.m.

He: Morning stretch and now off to the gym.
Have fun.

Me: How is the candle lighting ceremony in the square? I would love to be there with you.

Ah, distance.

He texts me hugs.

Good morning. Off to teach yoga.

He: Happy trails.

I am planning to visit him at his place.

I ask if there is anything he would like me to bring from my home.

He replies, nothing that I can think of. Thanks for asking.

And jokingly, I ask, what about me?

He said he knew that would be my response. Ha, ha.

This relationship in two different towns kept us at a distance. This was the same problem when I was married and this distance brought up many issues of sadness for me. I was not sure if this new relationship was sustainable with this distance and I wanted him to ask me to live in his town with him. He mentioned this but never took action. I finally bought a place there because I liked the town he lived in. He said this was okay, but I don't think he was happy with this move. It complicated things for him and he moved on.

He wishes us Merry Christmas, to me and the poodles. Just had a juice at the airport and I am feeling better.

I think you needed the hydration. Sorry, you didn't feel well last night.
Merry Christmas to you and yours.
I let him know I am halfway home.
And the gas stations are open.

He texts, he just got to Chicago.

I reply that I just got home.

He lands in New Jersey commenting that the weather is sunny and cold and that he slept most of the flight.

I continue the text—is your brother at the airport yet?

He texts back that he is waiting for his bag and that there is only one carousel for all flights—a zoo.

I wish him a glorious time with his family.
Have fun in New York City.
Smooch.

He: Good morning. 12 degrees here. Enjoy your day. Off to the city.

The train to New York is stuck; electrical issues and only one track open coming into NJ from Penn station.

He sounds frustrated so I remind him to breathe.
Did you arrive in NYC yet?

Yes. We had a nice lunch, then saw the Christmas windows at Macys. It is bitter cold here and going to get colder. Just not the weather to walk around in.

I text that I was having a lazy day.

And he comments, lazy days are good.

I hope you slept well.

He mentions he was up a few times due to trains and radiator heat sounds, then wishes me a good morning, continuing that he is looking forward to being back home. There is something about the wide-open spaces, beautiful vistas, clear mountain air, and skiing that makes life better.

What is on your agenda today?

I am walking on the wild side with the poodles.
We trudged through the golf course goose poop.
Spoke to a dear old friend struggling with loss.
I feel blessed.
I feel the joy of knowing you and keeping in touch.
Could use a hug about now.

He sends xoxo which was all he could do.
He tells me he just got back from bowling.
Since it is his brother's birthday, he let him win.
Tonight, pizza and beer.

I join in by text, happy birthday to your brother, and many more.

He thanks me and wishes me sweet dreams and says "night."
Another day in Jersey. Looking forward to getting home tomorrow and a good night's sleep.
His backpack is packed for Monday.

Greetings, dear sir, I know you will be busy from now until departure. Have a safe trip home with no delays.
You can text when you arrive home if you want to.

He says, Happy New Year missy.

Me: Don't forget traditional toe dip in the Atlantic!
He introduced me to his family and I thought he made me part of this family. I embraced them. I didn't realize this was a temporary situation which his family understood and I did not. I was removed from his family as quickly as I was introduced into it and then replaced. This was very difficult for me to understand and his family was used to his behavior.
I made split pea soup, an early lunch. The rest of the soup went into the freezer. Then, a spaghetti dinner.

He: Yum! Yum! Yum! Happy New Year. Off to the gym.
Then packing and to Newark airport.
All flights are on time and go.

Me: Happy trails! I am attempting to finish most paperwork for taxes. I am moving forward with the organization in the New Year.

There is a full moon this New Year, very special. You should have an amazing moon view while flying home.

Originally, I thought I would be driving him back to his house and we would celebrate the New Year. He chose to drive himself back and forth to the airport. I thought the New Year's moon was another sign from the universe that we were to be together; he did not see this opportunity either.

Did you make it to the airport?

He is ready to board his flight.
He says he is thinking of me.

Are you home yet?

He says he is on his way.
Happy New Year!
The tire was low and he had to find a gas station to fill it with air.

Poor kid, drive safely.

Made it home!
Real-time Happy New Year.
Sweet dreams.
Are you up?

CHAPTER 15

---~---

HIKING

He: Ice and heat on the leg! I went shopping at the pharmacy, saved 43%.

Me: Hope leg gets better soon. Since you have bruising, use arnica too.

My taxes are done on schedule!

He: How was your hike?

He mentions he should have taken a nap and that he will be a slug if he stays up until nine. He is returning to a different time zone.

I had a good New Year's hike. I hit a bit of a wall when I got back. The trails were all uphill and downhill with steep switchbacks of ice, snow, and mud.

I went with my neighbors. She and her husband are lovely.

They came over after we washed the mud out of our dogs and had champagne and cheese.

I am off to their home now for turkey soup.

xo.

He chats, just had a veggie burger with lettuce, tomatoes, and cheese, and ginger tea.

Tomorrow pancakes.

Me: Yum.

Wish I was on my way *(I wished he said please come).*

Good morning. Are you lazy this morning?

He just dropped the car off then walked home. Now, walking back to pick it up.

Pancakes were good this a.m.

He came back from New Jersey with a sore leg.

99% sure it is the abductor that is sore.

He has an appointment with the chiropractor.

Did you have a nail in your tire?

Hope the chiropractor gets your leg calmed down.

Yes, a rusty one.

Give it a tetanus shot!

Good yoga class today.

His chiropractor wants him to see an orthopedic surgeon; she said she has never seen this before.

I am sorry to hear that.

I am so annoyed the court date for the dog attack was postponed again.

He: Thank you for being you!

He is going to see his general practitioner tomorrow at 8:00.

Good luck with the doctor.

Keep me posted.

Too many reports from mom's lawyer. The system for delete is screwed up. Have to delete one message at a time, turn the phone off, then reboot. Otherwise, deleted message returns.

Nothing is simple.

Night.

He: It's only 8 pm.
Called to say goodnight.

Me: Mornin'.
Would you check to see if phone is straightened out and takes messages? Obviously, since upgraded, phone and computer are out of wack.
How are you feeling this morning?
Tried calling your phone and it doesn't appear to be on yet.

He is waiting for the doctor. He says he will get ultrasound next week if the leg is not better, but the swelling is down.
The doctor's conclusion is a bruised abductor.

That was our conclusion, we are so good.
Yoga and then lunch with my friend.
You make my heart sing. You make everything—groovy.
40 people in class today—not including me! A record-breaker.

He: You are hot!

Me: Feeling hot.
How was the book club?
Thought you were going to call?
Hope my phone is working.
(My frustration was he gives me a little and I am so crazy in love I think I hit the jackpot. It is me who is responsive and I melt if he gives me a little something at a distance. I react because this is too similar to how my husband treated me towards his end. This took three years for me to figure out what was going on with my chitchat buddy.)

Sweet dreams, missy.

Hey! Going to do my usual a.m. workout, read, and then heading out to the men's breakfast.

Sweet dreams.
Market run.
CPR class.
College basketball game.

He: Enjoy your class.
Are you through with your class?
Next day text from him, good morning.
Forecast 8" of snow for Taos Wednesday.

I will meet you in Taos? Ha, ha.
A storm is coming in tonight.
Coyotes are in the backyard in a pack early this morning, roaming.
Good yoga class.
How's the skiing?

He just iced the back of his knee.
He mentions he called me and tells me my box is full.
Getting later, heading to bed.
Miss you.
Night.
Sweet dreams.

Me: It rained last night then dusting of wet snow.
Yoga class yesterday. Forty-one people!
Poodle rebellion, not happy with walking in the wet snow.

He is getting boots fitted again.

I tell him that his boots don't sound like a good fit.

Lawn Ornament!

CHAPTER 16

STUFF

I am working on Mom's chaos.

I have phone calls to make this morning. She is in another panic because she ran out of her supplements and the company is not honoring her credit card; not sure how long this will take.

She gave the company the wrong numbers and forgot she was talking with her daughter—that's me. A bit scary. Might have to see her sooner than later. Of course, when I get there, most likely, everything will be fine.

I am going to a cleanse near his place. I wanted him to join me; he declined.

No police on the road.

Don't forget I need your time and place of birth for my teacher. I need data by Monday. He never gave the critical time. This was to help us with any pitfalls. *(I believe the truth is he would rather have the pitfalls so he could exit—again and again, his drama.)*

He: Good morning.
Eggs and grits for breakfast.
Off to do my a.m. stretches and then skiing.
Radio show at 3:30.

Me: Good morning, you are busy today.

He reports there is a storm coming in this weekend.
Have a great day.

I was on a cleanse diet for the five actions of cleansing the body, mind, and spirit.

He left me a message that he lost four pounds from my diet.

At least his comment left me laughing.
Congrats on your weight loss, sir.
I will be back to a normal diet by the weekend with a gentle food format. I still have a craving for guacamole!
Tonight's lecture is about atoms—coming together is creation; atoms leaving is aging and death.
Question: Why can't we work to understand keeping an atom together? Consciousness.
Another discussion he had no interest in.

Above my pay grade was his response.
Then, he discussed the weather.

My Poem
Not saying whether,
We will, whether we won't.
Whether it's long.
Whether it's short.
Nothing to see, nothing to expect.
Just the longer one knows one another,
The more exchanged,
The more shared.
Too much cleanse poetry? Just remember you lost 4 pounds!

His comment was your poem came out somewhat jumbled.
Not sure what you are saying.

Changing the subject, I ask how's the hip?
Enjoy your day.

Hip is hippy; thanks for asking.

I do enjoy hearing from you within your day.
My cleanse treatments really bring one to internal and external realizations.
Letting go.
Recharging.
Lightness.

He asks, how was the lecture?

Another great lecture, correlating times of day and night to organ health issues and quality times. It really makes sense.
Also, discussion of different tastes in your body through digestion and how food is assimilated—great bedtime stories.
Night.
Oh, how was the meatball and spaghetti dinner?

He responds, dinner was good.
Soak in the tub.
Went to bed early.
Had a reasonably good night's sleep.
Dreams, which I don't normally have.

I greet him with a good morning!
What kind of dreams?

He: Dreams. They came and left. Nothing remembered.

Me: Today is a wrap-up on treatments. See you at 3:30 for an early dinner.

I am really looking forward to seeing you.

Top of the morning to you.

The lecture is at 7 p.m.

Would you like to meet a bit later?

Ugh! Wish we had known sooner.

True. Apologies. *(Why am I always apologizing?)*

He did not have a good night's sleep and so he is a bit tired.

See you 4ish.

Did you just want to meet for the lecture?

And get there closer to 7 p.m., I will save you a seat.

No. See you 4ish.

I can meet you at the restaurant because it is closer to your exit with no backtracking and traffic.

No, he says he will meet me at the place I am staying and will drive us to the restaurant.

Running late, heavy traffic, says he.

Drive defensively.

XO.

He: Outside.

CHAPTER 17

POST CLEANSE

End of the cleanse. I am heading home.
I asked if I left my sweater at his house.

He did not find it.

My response—thanks for checking, will have to shave my
poodles and knit a new sweater, ha, ha!
No red dirt on my car from the drive, but I had to sweep out
the garage.
Very cold wind chill. It is minus 15. Sitting back, feet up,
chatting with my friend from Boston.
Phone connection terrible.
Sounds like I am underwater.
Help! Save me! Love cellphones. How did you know my sweater
turned up in my ski bag?
Thanks for the tip; never looked there.

He: Skiing was good.
Reading.
Soaking.
A meeting tonight.
Did you ski today?
Miss you.

No, I walked and walked.

Prepping for court—meditating. I am meeting the prosecutor tomorrow.

I am going up the mountain to organize the house for the sale.

Tomorrow, I have an early yoga class to cover for a colleague so she can go out of town.

Good evening, sir, there is space available for you on the river trip. Call the group leader if you would like.

Good night, he says, sweet dreams.

You too, dear one. Send my best to your friends.

Top of the mountain to you.

Late start, heading up the mountain to ski.

I am still throwing things away at the house. A friend and I are enjoying a glass of wine after dragging things around.

Are you almost done?

Reading.

Lights out.

I am walking the poodles and will be back in 15.

He: Will call then with lights out.

Good morning. Had breakfast, stretching, and then to the ski hill.

How is your knee?

Yikes, just woke up. Boys and I slept in. Slept till 8:30 too much dragging and hauling.

Knees stiff.

Dogs and I will walk the golf course so they can get their fill of goose poop, then ice, then hot bath.

Just had French toast and bacon.

Paying bills.

Making chicken soup.

Any topics for the radio show yet?

No topics yet. Just cleaning up and heading to do taxes.

Go sir, beautiful sunset.

Looking forward to seeing you Tuesday.

He says, me too!

I am taking a bath. My knee swelling is down.

Nite.

He: Good night and sweet dreams.

Me: You still can do the river trip and bring your son.

This is for your information and persuasion.

(Too stubborn, he did not join me. He did not even discuss why he did not want to go. He just avoided the discussion.)

He: Clean bill of health for choppers. Just finished with the dentist.

Go eagles! Got an interception when they needed it.

Had a good gym workout today.

Looking forward to tomorrow.

Good morning.

Have a great class.

Skiing was good today. Ten folks showed up.

Me: Wow, numbers are increasing like my yoga class.

He: How was your class?

Me: Different students today, more demonstrative. They wanted to be challenged and we did different positions.

He: A challenge for you, which makes it better for everyone. More adjustment on ski boots in town.

I walked my dogs.
The golf course melted; the grass is showing.
Paid bills.
Did three loads of laundry and cleaned the stove.

He wishes me a good morning. Powder day up to 13 inches today and tonight.
Off to stretch and then to the ski hill.
He continues, he needs to work out more and eat less when we are together. He says he put on two pounds. Have a great day.

Did you forget you lost 4 pounds on my diet!
No nibbles for you!
Have a great day.
Where did you put my house key?

Ugh! Jacket pocket. He has it. He says if I need it, he can express it back.

No worries, I will wait for the house cleaner. Glad to know it wasn't misplaced.

He: How about I come on the fifth and stay the week?

Me: I will be preparing for the river trip that week. You can help me pack!

It is a pleasure that we will be able to celebrate your birthday together.

He: Looking forward to seeing you and the poodles. Ski boots will last through this year. Still not happy with them. New boots and skis perhaps next year.

I just drove off a small embankment in a whiteout. Thank heaven for neighbors. They just drove me home.

Another neighbor will drive me to class tomorrow.

The emergency service can't get there until tomorrow afternoon. Not impressed with them for an emergency situation. If I had to wait in my car overnight in this isolated area, I could have frozen. Thank goodness for neighbors who care.

He texts, ugh! Glad everything is alright.

I am happy I am alright too. Hot chocolate and a thick piece of multi-grain bread for comfort food.

He: A cashmere sweater?

Me: Is that what you would like for your birthday?

He: No, a suggestion since you are chilled.

Me: I am choosing a hot bath.
Could really use you holding me right now.

He: I know what you mean. My thoughts are with you.
Enjoy the herb tea.
I am wiped out too. Heading upstairs.
Night.

Hope you are feeling better this morning. He just woke up.

He comments he had trouble sleeping.

I let him know the snow is deep. I hope I will be able to get the car out. Need to get my purse and credit cards out of the car at the very least.
Going to yoga then calling the emergency service.
Sorry to hear about the boots still not being right.
Hope your day is bright.
How's your back, shoulder, and knee?
Is the massage I gave you holding? (I am a massage therapist.)

He texts me the knee is good.
You worked magic on my back, etc.
Only four inches of snow.
Just called; didn't leave a message.

I am with an emergency truck. We have to find the car. Hopefully, it will be able to get towed.

You ok? The car has GPS. It is not lost.

Yes, I am. I will speak to you soon.
Hooray, we made it home. A sigh of relief.

CHAPTER 18

REPEAT, REMINDER

If one doesn't talk about things that bother one, things cannot be fixed. If one really cares and is committed to another, there is a discussion, not storming and introspection. With discussion, there can be resolution and being together. People work on imperfections to where they can be laughed at, worked with, or teased about lovingly.

If we really believe in commitment, we have to work together.

Men and women are different.

We all protect ourselves from fear and hurt.

Opening the door and letting someone in to expose who we really are requires trust through being open and not being afraid of discoveries whether good, bad, or neutral.

Getting hurt is no fun, but it is part of life. Shutting down keeps love away making one less than one can be. We do have a background that has to be shared in order to love again.

We win by sharing, being together, instead of being apart.

You were the judge and jury, hardly unbiased. You don't want to solve problems; you just want to complain about them. You don't want long-term sharing; you want temporary relationships.

For whatever reason, you need to find fault, not resolution. You want to blame the world; you want to blame me and not work on repairing either.

When it gets tough even at a meeting, you walk out. You don't want to hear the other side. You make the assumption you already know the other side.

You don't want to walk in someone else's shoes to try and understand. You feel you are the only one that knows what is right. You don't listen. You don't hear me. *(I made so much effort for him to try to hear me. My realization was that being together with someone shouldn't be that difficult.)*

Interestingly, I poured out my wisdom and he really didn't respond. Funny how I didn't get that he really didn't want commitment even though he said he did. I believed him. Why did he say one thing and then run away? I could not get an answer from him that I understood or could accept, which increased my frustration and my agitation.

He adds, sleep tight. Don't let the . . .
The next day, he is off to ski.
He texts me that he is with his church group. Always good.

I am going to look at new tents. I will be out of communication for twenty-one days. I want to make sure I have things in tip-top shape. It's like making sure you have the best shoes—no point in pain, concern, or discomfort.

I just saw a herd of elk on the golf course. They look like assorted lawn ornaments.

He tells me that he is in town getting new boots and skis. Then, he will be getting a bite to eat while he waits for the bindings to be mounted to the skis, etc. He should be finished by 7 p.m.

Assorted Elk Lawn Ornaments!

Happy birthday to you.
Call to tell me about your new purchases when you get home.
I just bought a two-person tent that is light and easy to set up.

He: Sweet dreams.

Me: You too.
Will walk poodles then sleep.
Enjoy your new toys.

He: Good morning. Decided to have pancakes and hit the gym.

Me: Found your sock.

He: I knew it was somewhere safe. Thank you.
Looking forward to Wednesday. Off to the gym.

Me: My client canceled. I went shopping for the river rafting trip. Got an updated solar-powered headlamp and ordered a solar charger.

The only sad in my happy is you chose not to come on this adventure.

I am going to college basketball games tonight.

Good games.

He: Glad you enjoyed the games. Going to the cinema to see the Bolshoi ballet, *Romeo and Juliet.* The cast is outstanding *(I longed to be with him to see the ballet together. I longed for him to ask me to be with him).*

Me: Enjoy the ballet. No one does it like the Bolshoi. It should be lavish.

Neighbors are coming over for dinner.

Hope you have enough tissues for the ballet.

Ski dreams to you.

He: No tissues needed.

Me: Brave soul.

He: Enjoy your dinner. Just finished two books and started a pile for the used book store.

A Good Salad For Dinner!

Me: Speedy reader.

He: How was dinner?

Me: Dinner was lovely,
Good morning.

He: Good morning to you.
Have a great class.
Making breakfast, then off to ski.
Just got home. Boots are good. Just need to ski a few more days in them to get them broken in.
Skis are ok. Need some mixed terrain and snow to really see their worth.

I didn't sleep well last night.
Had a hot chocolate so I was energized for class and worked students hard. Everyone was happy. Only about twelve people showed up. My students must have been up the mountain skiing.
In the evening, I continue, moon so bright, snow so white, easy to walk the doggies this night.
Do you want me to bring your blue jacket or leave it at my house?

He says please bring it.

There were twenty-two people in my yoga class today. It was a really good class.
How was skiing?

Skiing was good. A few more inches of snow fell.

Sweet dreams.

Good night missy.

Me: Good morning, steaming, then shower.
Poodle walk.
Bath.
Yoga.
Have fun today.

He says you too.
He just finished up skiing and asks how my yoga class was.

Yoga was good.
I am heading your way.
Lunch break stop, then on the road again.

He texts that he has wine, cheese, and crackers for my arrival.
(His next trip is to my place for his birthday)

Hey birthday boy, minus one day. Bring your snowshoes! Sweet dreams.

Sweet dreams to you too.
Think I am too tired to enjoy the awards.
Truth be told, I had two Guinness with my dawgs and kraut and beans.

You are a bad boy.
Hope you enjoyed them. Good night.

He thanks me for the singing telegram I sent for his birthday. He is on his way.

Drive with awareness, sir.

Almost there.

A massage awaits.

Thank you.

Organization and packing begin for my river trip.

Go gal!
Snowing here.
Typing up my radio notes.

Packing

I only have two bags left to pack.
Anything interesting in your notes?
Need me to proofread?
Movie, then some sleep.
Night.

He emailed me a copy of his notes.

Wow, good stuff.

Thank you.
Good night missy.

Me: How's the talk show going? It had to be great; your stuff was excellent.
The car is packed.

He: You are making progress.
How are you?

I made sure all is settled with mom before I take off for the trip. She panicked because she would not be able to get in touch with me for twenty-one days.
Funeral home payment is done, just in case.
Taxes, almost done.
Packing the final stuff now.
Five-hour drive mostly through Native American country.
I left a message for mom's lawyer with your phone number.

He: Cute. How is your evening?

Me: Doing laundry.
Shower, steam, and bath before my 5 a.m. departure!!
How is your evening?

He: Enjoy.
Watch your speed.

Me: Last bath for three weeks.

He: Nite missy.

Me: Nite dear sir.

CHAPTER 19

~

RETROSPECTION

When he had the horror of losing his son, I was there for him.

I took calls in the wee hours even when I had to work when his son was dying. I picked him up at the airport at midnight when he returned so he wouldn't be alone. I had to drive 250 miles back home at 4 a.m. to teach my early morning class. He said that was crazy to do, but I wanted to support him. I talked to his brother about what was going on. He did not want me to be with him during this time. I left caring presents at his home to help soften his pain when he returned. I left a good meal he didn't eat.

I really don't think he appreciated any of this. It is true he said it was ridiculous for me to come for such a short time, but my heart did not want him to be alone.

He was unable to understand when I was under stress with fires near my home or his departures that reminded me of death since my husband died and never came home again.

He stormed out and left me once again.

I thanked him for being who he was and getting me through my mother's crazies.

I finally get that my mother's love is conditional as was his. This is a trait for self-centered people—a struggle for me.

She gets me stuck in old stories that I am finished with, as did he.

When I feel good and competent, my mother knows how to make me feel worthless. He does not do this, but he does remove my strength when we can't talk face to face and when he avoids my questions through evasion or walking out.

It hurts when they do their variations of hurt.

I then relate to others poorly because I feel I am not of value.

I appreciated him stepping up to the plate and taking care of me during a number of mother crises. This warmed my heart at so many different levels. I thought he was on my team. I thought he was my partner, but he was not capable of being with me as a consistent partner.

I have to remember my mother was not a gentle person; she pretended to be and this was the definition of mother crazies for me.

One time, he stood by me. He did not buckle under my mother's force. He was there for me.

Stop The Confusion, The Storm Will Pass

And then, he walked out again with no discussion, no explanation—something he said he would do to avoid the drama, but his storming off was the drama. This happened over and over again. The drama was his and I didn't get it.

He returned when I needed someone's support. He stayed with me for forty days when I had rotator cuff surgery. Unfortunately, he could not tolerate someone else's pain. He tried. He did this by talking about his past injuries. He did not know how to be empathetic, to just listen, to comfort, to rub one's back, to hold someone's head, and to offer words of kindness. He was just there, not present but there.

Again, I poured my heart out to him and he treated me poorly with his storming off. He really had no understanding of me and yet, he carelessly said he did.

Thank heaven I teach where people listen and respect me. My mother and he knew how to reduce me to rubble. I recognized this trait in him because of how my mother treated me. I thought I would be able to be strong enough to deal with his reactions because I thought I understood where he was coming from. I was not strong enough. The good stuff in our relationship was not strong enough.

I received a 6 a.m. pre-evacuation call for fire and flooding near my home! I was scared.

Fire!!!

My thoughts went to losing my home to fire. When we had a pre evacuation warning, I drove to his home. He asked me to leave because I was upset *(Why couldn't he just hold me to calm me down? That was all I needed.)*

Air quality was bad at home.

I returned home at 2 a.m.

I texted him that I appreciated him letting me rest there briefly at his home before I left. I said it helped stabilize me for the drive home. *(At least, it was something. Once again, I accepted only crumbs.*

To repay him, I invited him to stay at my home while renters stayed at his. He accepted this offer. I seemed to offer him too much for his brief moments of kindness.)

He texted, glad you made it home safely. Wishing you the best always.

No talk?

Done?

He: Yes.

(Why did I have to ask? He could never give me closure. He would vacillate from seeming to care to distancing.)

Me: I certainly will miss you. Health and joy.

Just Across The Street From My Home

I could not understand how he seemed to disregard my concerns about the fires near my home and my emotional stress; he just said I was out of control.

He continued, the last couple of days of "talk and actions" took care of everything.

(He shut down. He did not want to console me; his choice; his drama was an exit.)

He blamed me for the disruption of his life. He blamed me for drama, not the fires. He blamed me for being out of control instead of being empathetic and trying to comfort me.

How could I have wanted to prolong such a lopsided relationship? Why did I think so little of myself? *(Because when he was with me, it was nice being with him.)*

She understood that emotions were an expression of one's utmost vulnerability to share with someone that could be trusted.

He understood expressed emotions as pathological reactions, which would allow him to stay at the periphery of the relationship making it easy for him to exit.

Message from La Plata county:
Hermosa evacuation orders lifted.

CHAPTER 20

COMMITMENT

Booking things in advance does not indicate commitment as we can clearly see.

Commitment is expressing one's thoughts outside of the mind so another human can hear instead of watching TV to numb thoughts. My deceased husband did this through his clinical depression.

Was this happening again with a variation? Sometimes, when I needed his holding for comfort, he sat in bed on his cellphone. It was difficult watching him turn away when closeness was needed.

If two people don't discuss what is going on emotionally, the dissolution of a relationship occurs. How did I miss that I was involved and he was not? I always had questions because I could not understand his closeness followed by distancing. I speculated because I could get no answers from him. He was unable to give me full disclosure about himself; no trust.

I was uncomfortable asking him questions because my questions were not answered—only parlayed with other questions or no answer at all. This made me upset. This created tension. I tried so hard to make him hear me and he did not. I so wanted to hear what he had to say.

I was so disappointed when he backed away from the discussions he said he wanted to have.

His actions seem to be the opposite of what he said and didn't say.

I thought we were good friends, but friends do not treat friends poorly.

I am training myself to let go of everything I fear to lose.

My last-ditch effort, another futile attempt, as I continued to ignore "what is."

My plea.
Do open your heart.
Don't throw us out.
We do have some pleasant interactions together.

CHAPTER 21

REALIZATIONS

I think I tried to be tolerant of him because I did not have this opportunity with my sick husband.

My question: Since we know I get anxious close to either of our departures, is it possible for you to be able to be kinder/gentler to me rather than reactive? Perhaps, you should realize I will miss you that much.

Of course, he delayed his response with his first comment "enjoy your yoga class."

Then, he continued later that I should be more in control of the situation. *(He always countered; he always blamed; he never wanted to share responsibility.)*

I said again with your support and kindness, control can happen. I need to know you will be there when things get tough and in turn, I will be there for you.

He continued to be incapable of giving me what I needed. He did not want to be there for anyone except himself.

He went into his own world and merely said, enjoy your day!

(I didn't give up, was I so desperate? Why did I think I could make him hear? I tried so hard in futility with false hope and he let me do this. I had training from my mother and from my deceased husband. I tried

so hard—incomplete training. I did not know how to let go. I seemed to have chosen to punish myself. I just could not accept someone could be so dense or so uncaring.)

And then he texts me as if nothing had occurred.

He says, ignoring my frustration, a friend and I are getting together tomorrow.

I was so happy to hear his chitchat I tried to forget my hurt.
Should we think about a picnic?

He gives me a thumbs up for the picnic.
And says good morning, missing you.
Then, in the evening, he wishes me sweet dreams.
How did this happen again? How did we get back together again after all of this?

How could I be that forgiving? Why would I want to torture myself like this? Why did I want to believe in someone who couldn't hear me? Why did I try so hard? Why was I so determined to keep this relationship going? Very incomplete training from dealing with my self-centered mother.

I say sweet dreams.

More chatter from him, woke up tired. Ugh.
Had the usual breakfast and everything is ok.
Heading to Tent Rocks.

I tell him to enjoy the magic!
Great, not great, back in the story.
I ask more questions:
I know you have spoken about who you thought was the love of your life.

Are you through with that idea? Do you think it might ever happen again? *(Why do I keep asking these questions only to get no answers? Why was I so determined to get blood from a stone?)*

Can we plan on hiking too?

He: We can't do Tent Rocks with the dogs, but we can do badlands. We need to go early; old ruins hike is ok too.

His answer or should I say his sarcasm from my previous questions: the first love of my life was my first fire truck, a pair of ice skates, my bike, my first car, and then . . .

Me: Come on, stop your flip answers to my questions. Stop. Not cute.

I am referring to your seventeen-year travel companion, your wife, or did I misunderstand you that evening and you truly were talking about your fire truck, skates, bike, and first car?

I ask again, being determined, are you looking for another love of your life in human form or are you just biding your time until your endgame?

(I believe his desire was to try all variations of women without commitment. He was unable to be honest with himself or others.)

Yet another avoidance of an answer from him.

Have you been reading Freud?

If so, please stop.

Off to shop.

We can discuss this later.

(Why am I taking this?)

In my disappointment, I made light of another sarcastic response to me.

Ha, ha, I said instead of cutting him loose.

Have fun shopping, I said, covering my exasperation.

I do look forward to a discussion later. I continued with false hope.

All I wanted was to get to know him better.

We did this story already.

He pushed my patience to the maximum.

I always tried to be patient with other people's lack of kindness.

Again, incomplete training from my mother.

I tried so hard to receive the love from her that I needed.

I bent until I broke.

This is happening again.

I answered the questions I asked him.

What am I doing to myself?

Why am I tormenting myself?

This was incomplete training from my mother.

It is time to let it go.

But I continue.

I actually answer my own question to him:

You asked me what I think you want in a relationship—

someone you feel sparks with,

someone who makes you think,

someone who likes many of the things you do,

someone who treats you special,

someone who is financially independent,

someone who likes to travel.

Seems like that is on par with what you would like in a relationship?

Am I on the right track?

(I thought I fit the bill so I wanted him to see this—my delusion, my false hope, my training to be subservient to someone who is self-centered and I continue to ignore my needs. Realization: let go of this training. It is not good for me.)

In truth, he turned my need for answers about us into a general discussion. This just frustrated me so.

He gave me a thumbs-up, approving my answer.

Then somewhat, without any specifics, he continues to be divisive.

Ok, then what are you specifically looking for?

Am I part of your idea of a long-term relationship or a shorter one?

(I took another round of his avoidance, abuse. How well I was trained. Let the training go!)

Again, he is evasive. If he just answered my questions in the first place, there would be a much more peaceful relationship. I would be less stressed. His evasions did not amuse me. They hurt me deeply.

I suppose he felt if I stopped asking questions, we would have a much more peaceful relationship.

Stalemate.

So, what does your "somewhat" comment mean since I described what I thought you want in a relationship?

Yes, I am persistent.

Not a good trait in this situation, but I wanted answers.

Instead, he replies questioning me.

He talks about my dogs.

Lack of sleep.

And then he asks me questions, which do not answer my questions about the relationship.

How do you see yourself, he asks.

(Does he just like pricking a wound as my mother did?

I think he just liked off-centering me.

Why does he do this?

Did he want me to exit as he does?

He always exited if I asked too many questions. I never thought of this before. I dug in.)

What do you want in a relationship? He asks, continuing to avoid answering my questions and he wonders why my frustration builds. He is a master interrogator and I innocently and thoughtfully answer his questions.

Thinking about your questions, they are important ones. Are you seeking superficial answers or answer from the heart?

He continues to torment me—good question a third option—practical, or however you choose to answer.

(I didn't see the replay, the story he kept me in. I kept hoping he would open up to me and he never would. He was a master manipulator to get what he wanted and not give what someone else needed.)

I am still waiting for your translation of "somewhat" in terms of what you need in a relationship with *someone*. He could not acknowledge me.

What is acceptable and unacceptable?

He says he will answer my questions tomorrow morning; tired and trying to stay awake.

Wow, he dangles another carrot in front of me and I accept with patience. But my patience is running out and I didn't even understand he was worse than my mother in undermining me and trying to destroy my love, my kindness, and my honesty.

And so, I answer his questions.

Writing items down makes me realize there is so much more as thoughts and actions are appearing and disappearing daily.

I do know it would give me great pleasure to define a relationship, specifically with you, because you are the one I would like to be in a relationship with.

I answer these questions because these questions will actually help me understand myself and what I need in a relationship:

- enjoying physical closeness in all ways.
- sharing chores.
- enjoying dining in and out together.
- fearlessly expressing ideas, thoughts, and information in agreement and disagreement with discussion and respect, not

watching someone storm off because he no longer controls the situation but shares it *(this was our downfall)*.
- enjoy exercising together.
- enjoy sharing family together.
- enjoy local and distant adventures together.
- creating our memories with each other.

How I see myself:

I am independent yet I enjoy working with others as well as having someone do something for me out of caring.

I enjoy exploring, playing, and being physically close to someone I trust and have deep feelings for.

When I do care deeply for someone who is also on my side, I will stick by them through good and bad, joy and grief. *(This was my training in the relationship with my mother who didn't try to get along with me. It was her way or no way. I still tried to get along.)*

I am passionate about life and love being able to share life experiences.

I take great pleasure in observing and listening to different ideas and opinions which help me learn.

I am grateful for good health.

Again, as I write things down, there is so much more of me and ideas about relationships.

He comments I can't read anything; text was too long.

I spent a great deal of time thinking about your questions you asked me and I responded carefully and all you have to say was you couldn't read anything because my text was too long? I can read it to you.

Ok, and says he will call me when he is home from the book club around 8 p.m. *(I notice he chooses to get to me at his convenience, not mine.)*

By the way, I still haven't received your "somewhat" answer.

Finally, because of my persistence, he texts somewhat—what I am looking for is *someone* who enjoys being loved and who is interesting to talk to. Anything else is gravy.
Good night, missy.

Me: Exhausted, this is like pulling teeth to get answers from him. He uses *someone,* not specifically me. What a tease. Good night, sir.

He: Awake. Hope to get back to sleep.

Me: How ya feeling? Wonder what woke you up?

He: Our discussion last night.
Just finished up at the gym.

Me: What do you mean?
What was your concern?

He: No concern. I told you what I was looking for and you twisted it around and made it into a drama, and neither one of us needs drama in our lives. *(He twists and I defend myself.)*

I am sorry. *(I can't believe I apologized)* I continued I did not twist the text. To me, it clearly stated *someone.* To me, that is a general statement that may or may not be me.
I thought I had expressed thoughts about our relationship and it felt like you stepped back from you and me to general.
If you don't want misunderstandings, be clear, not vague. Talk about you and me, not *someone.*
I have absolutely no intention to create drama. I just wanted clarification.

Sorry, you didn't get it. *(Again, I say I am sorry. I shouldn't be sorry; he is the one that twisted the whole of our relationship. Let go of this mother training.)* True, we do not need drama unless it is opera!

He: At car dealer for an oil change *(back to his world.)*.
You are a wonderful person with a heart of gold.
What happened is something you cannot control. It is spontaneous. There is nothing to forgive. But I do forgive "us." *(The man is way out of line.)*

(There was no need to defend myself to him yet I still tried to get him to hear me, continued futility.)
It is not a spontaneous reaction, it evolves from my frustration about our miscommunication, lack of communication, and no communication between us.

He: And we can leave it at that, wanting his words to be the last.

Me: No, if you didn't want to work on our relationship, to move it toward a positive direction, why did you meet with a therapist? We both needed a good coach to work on our reactions and cooperation.
Why did you invest in this facilitation?
Working for both of us takes time and patience for change, which can be done if both parties want to emotionally invest, share honestly and openly, and trust.
Hell, you could have invested in a new full-price pair of ski pants and not wasted my time with you!

He: No response. *(I am beginning to step back and observe.)*

Me: My dream is to be with someone now in these times of pandemic, crisis, and in times of peace.
I did the distance stuff with my deceased husband and I need the richness of a partnership.
The distance reminds me of what I don't want.

The therapist made an effort to improve our relationship.

You only wanted to make things better for yourself.

Working together is the secret of a partnership. If you had chosen to work together, we would have been together, not apart.

I am stopping this now.

This man survived through reactivity, not response-ability, leading him down the path of non-productivity in this relationship.

I got it!

I got it!

I got it!

Just working on my shoulders and my heart right now.

February Snow Moon

My thoughts for him:

It is funny that what you see and feel is not what someone else sees and feels, yet you believe they do. You don't see this until you get "what is."

Had you ever counted how many rainbows we saw together?

I thought this was a sign from the universe.

It thrilled me to share these rainbows with you but all you said was they were only a scientific phenomenon.

This hurt my heart.

I counted many full moons we saw together.

Those meant nothing to you for us.

This pained my heart.

I saw romance and signs from the universe we were meant to be together.

You saw nothing.

My heart broke.

I tried to make you see me, see us. You saw nothing worth working for.

You say I didn't understand how your heart hurt.

I did understand, I wanted to be with you and you didn't want to be with me.

My heart is smashed. I never felt like we should end. But you ended it.

I have difficulty understanding how two people see things so differently when I thought we shared a loving vision. We did not.

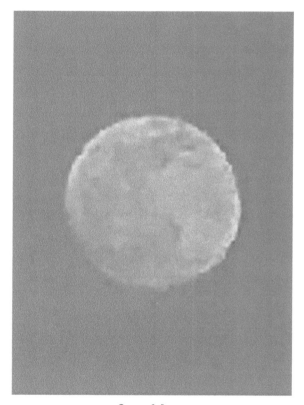

Snow Moon

He texts what I wrote was eloquent, more later. *(His modus operandi was a pat on the head and then offering torment with his delayed response.)*

He texts again rainbows—did I count them? No.

Yes, it was meaningful seeing them with *someone*. Nature at work is a joy to behold, especially when you are with *someone* you care for. The same holds true for sunrises, full moons, sunsets, a snow-capped mountain . . . To say nothing matters to me . . .

If this mattered, you would have held it in your heart, not stress. You would have acknowledged me, not *someone*.

Your heartburn was a reaction to you doing something wrong.

You left a pot burning on the stove. Due to my injury, I could not lift the pot off the fire. I panicked. I sought your help; I could not move the pot at that moment. I called you in lower tones. You did not hear me. My volume increased.

He says his body does what it does. And it goes into stress mode when you end up doing your thing, which you can't control nor know it is coming. *(He convinces only himself he has no responsibility for actions and reactions. Let this go, I say to myself, incomplete training by my mother.)*

I tried very hard to please my mother as a child, which was futile.

She did not want to accept who I was. I could only please her if I did what she wanted me to do.

My expression of love was unacceptable to her.

I was used to not being heard and not being allowed to express myself.

He: How are you? How are your shoulders? How are the dogs?

The end of communication almost . . .

Ahhh The Rainbow the Connection with the Universe

Quote from Brahma Kumaris' lecture 4/11/2020, Enhance Your Spiritual Immunity:

"We don't have any control on the outside circumstances but what we have control is on our inner state.

If our inner strength is strong, we can respond to the situation rather than react to the situation.

Reaction happens if we are under the influence of the situation.

Response is that which comes from our inner strength from a state of being powerful.

If we are weak, the situation becomes strong.

If we are a little strong, the situation becomes a challenge.

If we are strong enough, the situation becomes an opportunity."

He: How are your shoulders doing? *(Why is he asking? Why is he trying to engage me in conversation again? My answer to me, because I continue to respond.)*

Me: I am holding deep-seated grief because of your poorly executed departure.
I had a tough dream.
Fortunately or unfortunately, this is one I remember vividly.
I slipped and was hanging off a cliff.
I called you for help to pull me up.
You stood there and watched me fall.

He: Dramatic comes to mind.
It was a full moon.
According to a psychology course I took, one does not die in one's dreams.

Me: You missed the point.
Obviously, I didn't die.
Death of a partnership does come to mind. The reality of the end of our relationship was identified.

He: Just called you.

Me: I am at physical therapy for my shoulder until 1 p.m. Call if you would like.

It was 1:50 and he never called back.

A quote from Gilgamesh, page 52, *Gilgamesh* by Stephen Mitchell, copyright 2004, 2005, CPJ group (UK):

> "We cannot accept things as they are so long as we think things should be different"
> *(This is what I have to work on.)*

Gilgamesh, continued page 52:

> "Tell us how not to believe what we think and then maybe we will be able to hear."
> *(This is what he has to work on.)*

My actions were the result of your actions. Your reactions were the result of my reactions.

He: What is to be gained discussing this again. *(True when you are not open, there is no point. When you cannot hear, there is no point. When there is no face to face discussion, there is no point.)*

Me: I have shared; you were silent.
Again, discussion requires two parties in dialogue, face to face.
Actually, we really didn't hear each other.
Sad, I thought we did.
I thought you/we hired a facilitator to better understand each other and know our love, health, happiness, peace, and joy with each other and put the frustration and anger into the garbage.
It is obvious when I am upset and respond to your lack of response, this sets things in motion for both of us.

He: True.

Me: It tears me apart when you can't hear me and ignore me.
That is why I thought your suggestion of the facilitator would help us, but you bailed.
I need time to unlearn reactions and so do you.
You don't even care to work on you.
It is always someone else's fault.
You continue to blame others.
You continue to take no responsibility.
I thought the therapist would help.
Instead, you threw me under the wheels of a truck.
You think you are honest but you are not honest with yourself.
It is ironic you exited to your home to see places, ski with friends, and be with other friends and the pandemic came and you were alone. We could have ridden the storm together. Sad when you

left, you didn't even check up on me and my recovery—and you said you cared. What garbage.

You never inquired, you just moved on.

He: I got it. I apologize.

Me: I should have recognized with your failed relationships, the failures included two people.

Your parents stayed together for many years because they wanted to be together.

There are two different people in a relationship and no matter how much you care for each other there are differences. You have to forgive.

You did not want to do the hard homework.

The tragedy of it all is how many boys are never taught to understand emotions. They are taught to stifle their emotions; they are slapped and yelled at to learn not to hear themselves.

In response or reaction they begin to ignore, dislike or undermine women for expressing their emotions. The boys become men and are shut down.

I had the surgery and in your drama, you had the pain.

You need to open your heart. Embrace the tightness because you cannot empathize with someone else's pain.

He: I just read through all your texts and I will answer you in the morning. The stove incident felt like a heart attack coming on when you yelled *(here we go again)*. I walked over to you and my whole body knotted. *(Again, you took no responsibility for burning up a pot I could not move. It is always you, you, you.)*

When I left, another incident *(yes, and after that you held me)*.

Time to move on.

You were dishonest with yourself and me. You accepted my apologies for the stove yell.

When you have to work on something, even if it has the possibility to be worthwhile, you move on.

You hide in your mind.

The tightness in your heart will continue in all of your relationships because you leave before you make an effort to understand.

You are stuck and don't want to be unstuck.

You move on to a new relationship so you will not have to reveal too much of yourself.

When you open up, your next step is to exit for fear of getting hurt again.

He: You are making everything dark. It was not.

I respond, when you can't work on things with your partner and when you have no more opportunity with someone you care for, your rejection and distancing of everything is pretty darn dark.

He: How are your shoulders doing?

The Moon Rises In Darkness

CHAPTER 22

CHITCHAT AND ALL OF THAT

I think we can all understand the chitchat was fun.

He and I could talk about health, hiking, skiing, family, politics, weather, food, and humor.

The difficulty was if something came up that was upsetting to him, he left with no explanation.

No one is perfect in a relationship.

There are times when one upsets the other incurring anger, exits, and explosions.

In these moments, love and kindness vanish.

This upset is not the mainstay of the relationship however and must be put in perspective if a long-term relationship is intended.

Keep the good stuff.

Release the bad.

Let it go.

CHAPTER 23

ONE DEAD ONE LIVING

One dead + one living = 1 dead + 1 living

I was never given an opportunity to self-correct, to make things better, to improve, to become a better person, or to enjoy the relationship with better understanding.

He chose not to accept the opportunity to self-correct, to make things better, to become a better person, or to enjoy a relationship with better understanding.

Choosing the wrong people causes pain and suffering.

I am in search of someone who wants to work together.
Step over the threshold of past relationships.

The ultimate truth is we are born, we live, we die.
It is up to each of us and the universe how we spend our time between birth and death.
We may choose universal truth, non-judgment, compassion, and unconditional love.
Or we can choose worldly truth where there is judgment, selfishness, conditional love, and hate.

His attempt at being a caretaker was not one of his natural roles though it was appreciated.
Being a patient was not my natural role either.
These were not our better moments.

We both needed to step back in observation.

We must observe ourselves, our responses, and our reactions without emotional involvement.

The neutral observations permit us to see what is really going on.

"Observe the observer observing the observed."

Life is not a quick fix.

We need to acknowledge the worst of us and the best of us.

We need to work on the best parts and understand where the worst parts are coming from so the negative can come to rest.

The dead partner internalized sadness, frustration, and anger which caused clinical depression.

The living partner externalized sadness, frustration, and anger which caused reactivity.

I was derailed by both of these relationships because of how I was trained to accept unacceptable behavior from self-centered people.

CHAPTER 24

CARING?

My thoughts on caring are accepting, understanding, and offering another chance.

Caring is having the strength to work things out.

One's brain without a heart is unfulfilling and empty.

With no heart and mind connection one becomes ill.

A relationship must be with no judgment, with problem-solving to work on joy and sorrow, pain and pleasure, love and hate, and agreements and disagreements.

We all need to work from an open heart and mind sharing the past, present, and future in non-judging, unconditional love.

The definition seems simple.

Action is challenging.

Understanding is healing.

Making an effort to change is difficult without reaction, just responsiveness.

The reward—heart and mind connection offering peace, love, and relationship.

After all, we are social beings.

He responds, the seeds of our relationship burned with the episode at the kitchen stove and my reaction to it. A stress filled my body, which encapsulated my heart, and which felt like a heart attack coming on.

The ashes? They were blown away and joined our loved ones in space.

It is past time for both of us to move on.

Wishing you health and happiness in all that you do. Always.

(Is it healthy to keep the door open for him? To return at his convenience?

No.

It is healthy if one wants to return and try to understand with discussion face to face, answering questions honestly.

Do I want to wait for this man?
No.

One cannot wait if there is no response.

He began dating someone else immediately.
He is gone.
His pattern is of a serial dater with longer and shorter term relationships.

I wanted to evolve through this relationship.

He continues to try all the cookies in all the cookie jars.)

CHAPTER 25

TRASH CANS FULL OF
DISCARDED MEMORIES

I don't want to be judged; I want to be loved.

We are all on a personal struggle to understand who we are.

The relationship I had with my mother was challenging, making her one of my best teachers.

As I look back, I think my mother subjugated me to keep me off balance.

Because of her narcissistic personality, she kept me from the realization of myself and compromised my feelings.

As long as I was subservient to her, my mother accepted me.

My lesson is that being determined in what I do and who I am is important. However, trying to convince others who are self-involved is a futile act.

My mother, my husband, and my friend were narcissistic, arrogant, and self-absorbed, ranging from illness to unpleasant communication and lack of communication.

This type of personality makes it impossible for mutual communication.

This creates an unhealthy situation.

I tried to take on impossible tasks with my mother.

I tried to please her. I tried to share my perspective.

When these things could not be shared, I tried harder.

My efforts in communication were futile.

This futility made me feel bad.

I could not accept that it was impossible for me to succeed with someone who had a self-centered personality.

Trying harder caused me more pain.

My next lesson is to be who I am and let these people be who they are.

There are no apologies necessary.

The emotional generosity I offer to others must also be offered to myself.

I must learn that I do not have to pay with tolerance to receive love.

How willing am I to be aware of what I no longer want to put up with?

I need to be heard.

You need to be heard.

We all need to be heard.

CHAPTER 26

MY ROMANTIC VISION

My dreams—

I want to be with you daily from sunrise to sunset to sunrise again.

I want to share the complexities of life.

I want to be engaged with you mentally, physically, spiritually, emotionally, intellectually, and lovingly.

I want a symbol shared, representing unending hope, love, support, non-judgment, compassion, and passion together.

I want laughter, tears, and holding each other physically, mentally and spiritually.

I want you to be there in comfort and discomfort, sharing understanding and not understanding, agreeing and disagreeing, and accepting, all of that.

(I presented this note to him. He never told me he read this until I asked him if he did. When he responded that he read it, several weeks later, he said nothing.

I was prepared to commit myself to him.

He was not prepared to commit himself to me.

I could no longer see my life without him.

He was only interested in someone, not me.)

CHAPTER 27

CALM

I feel calm with truth and acceptance.

Then, my mind teases me and moves me to the future of worry and what might happen.

My mind doesn't want me to be in the present moment.

I witness the doubting mind of what-ifs, would-haves, could-haves, and should-haves.

I must move the ego of the mind to *what is* by creating calm.

Accepting that what is, is what is!

CHAPTER 28

AFFIRMATIONS

Our positive thoughts (from Brahma Kumaris' lecture *Sailing Through Turbulent Times* 5/23/2020)—

These are affirmations that can help us move on to a better connection with ourselves, with others, and with the universe:

I am a powerful being. This power gives me strength.

I am a peaceful being. This peace creates internal calm.

I am a fearless being. This fearlessness protects me from the fear around me.

My body is perfect and healthy and always will be.

(No what-ifs.)

The universe offers me, my family, my friends, my work and my planet power and blessings making a circle of protection around us.

When I first wake up, I give peace to myself through these positive thoughts and exercise.

I do these affirmations before I watch the news or look at the cellphone or television.

Before bed, I turn off the television, cellphone, and news and allow these positive thoughts to give me relaxation before sleep.

CHAPTER 29

OBSERVATIONS

Women usually have more training as nurturers, while men are better known to be hunters and gatherers.

It seems some men are able to compartmentalize relationships and move on, while some women try to understand what was happening in the relationship, which can prevent women from moving on easily.

Some women receive negative imprints about themselves growing up in their families, while men are usually encouraged with more positive support.

As women, we must stop asking what is wrong with us.

We must forgive ourselves.

We must see ourselves before we see ourselves from eyes that are not our own.

In a relationship, we can be in different places.

We need emotional generosity for one's self and for others.

We need to understand some people hear us and others do not.

We need to share uninterrupted thoughts.

We need to be heard.

Change is constant.

We must know who we are.

One needs clarity from another and in turn, one needs to be clear.

We need to take the responsibility of responding.

We all have hurt.

It is important to be respectful of someone else's sensitivities.

Every human is impacted by past experiences.

What informs us right now is who we are and what we need.

No blame, not even blaming one's self.

We need to be willing to open and grow.

We all have a part in what is going on.

There is a difference in having our needs met, rather than meeting our wants and desires.

We need to pay attention to what we want, pay attention to what we need, and know what is.

In relationships, we learn from our past experiences, live in our present, and let our future be developed from this awareness.

CHAPTER 30

~

WITH LOVE

Through many years of seeing myself through the eyes of others
— I have seen myself through my mother as not pretty; through
my father with the impossibility to have a fulfilling artistic career;
through my husband who overlooked my needs; through my friend
who wrote me off as out of control. I suppressed me, by believing
what others thought of me.

I tried to accept that these outsiders knew me better than myself,
so I struggled.

By looking through the eyes of others we become aliens to
ourselves creating negative images which push others away.

The opposite of what we want.

Incomplete training.

I realize now I must see myself through my eyes.

Through my eyes, I see myself as intelligent, thoughtful, athletic,
spiritual, a sexual being and creative, which makes me whole.

Our guidance must come from within.

We must let go of other people's visions of us.

We must learn to accept ourselves with strengths and weaknesses,
consistently observing ourselves to avoid self doubt and guilt.

We need to remember to use our own eyes for love, honesty and
courage for ourselves.

With respect for ourselves we become valuable, unique and lovable.

We need to practice this.

CHAPTER 31

---~---

CONCLUSION

A quote from Learning by Jorge Luis Borges, translated by Blanca Zarsan from an app Lost in Translation https://translationwanderer.tumbir.com

"After some time, you learn the subtle difference between holding a hand and imprisoning a soul;

You learn that love does not equal sex, and that company does not equal security, and you start to learn...

That kisses are not contracts and gifts are not promises, and you start to accept defeat with the head up high and open eyes, and you learn to build all roads on today, because the terrain of tomorrow is too insecure for plans...and the future has its own way of falling apart in half.

And you learn that if it's too much even the warmth of the sun can burn.

So you plant your own garden and embellish your own soul, instead of waiting for someone to bring flowers to you.

And you learn that you can actually bear hardship, that you are actually strong, and you are actually worthy, and you learn and learn... and so every day.

Over time you learn that being with someone because they offer you good future, means that sooner or later you'll want to return to your past.

Over time you comprehend that only who is capable of loving you with your flaws, with no intention of changing you can bring you all happiness.

Over time you learn that if you are with a person only to accompany your own solitude, irremediably you'll end up wishing not to see them again.

Over time you learn that real friends are few, and whoever doesn't fight for them, sooner or later, will find himself surrounded only with false friendships.

Over time you learn that words spoken in moments of anger continue hurting throughout a lifetime.

Over time you learn that everyone can apologize, but forgiveness is an attribute to great souls.

Over time you comprehend that if you have hurt a friend harshly it is very likely that your friendship will never be the same.

Over time you realize that despite being happy with your friends, you cry for those you let go.

Over time you realize that every experience lived, with each person is unrepeatable.

Over time you realize that whoever humiliates you or scorns another human being, sooner or later will suffer the same humiliations or scorn tenfold.

Over time you learn to build your roads on today, because the path of tomorrow doesn't exist.

Over time you comprehend that rushing things or forcing them to happen causes the finale to be different from expected.

Over time you realize that in fact the best was not the future, but the moment you were living just that instant,

Over time you will see that even when you are happy with those around you'll yearn for those who walked away .

Over time you will learn to forgive or ask for forgiveness, say you love, say you miss, say you need, say you want to be friends, since before the grave it no longer makes sense..."

When tears pass and the tempest of rage dies,
we discover the love in our hearts keep us alive.

With gratitude to those behind-the-scenes friends that
helped me hone a rough manuscript into the book
And Then He Kissed the Dog, A Fine Break Up:

Leslie
Pat
Martin
Betsy and Phil
Bob
Lizzie
Deborah and Elmer
Jo
Christine
Donna
Janet S
April, Liz
Erik

Thank you for offering me insight.
Some of you reading and re-reading the pile
of papers that turned into a book!

CPSIA information can be obtained
at www.ICGtesting.com
Printed in the USA
BVHW051203020921
615902BV00020B/884

9 781956 010220